C. Hammond

11-16 08

To Bertha —
The best of the BEST —
Love always,

the Creative Journey

Copyrighted 2006 - Library of Congress

ISBN # 0-9779529-0-8

Published in Washoe Valley, NV
Vivian Hammond
2950 White Pine Drive
Washoe Valley, NV 89704

the Creative Journey

Volume 2   *2006*

the Creative Journey is happening once again. Our first attempt in 2003 was a surprising success in that it turned out to be a beautiful book of which I personally was very proud. The contributors and others who actually bought the book thought very highly of it and so here we are again hoping that you all enjoy our continued and loving efforts. As before I know from experience what a lonely and wonderful path you take when you choose to write. However, someone once said that after you learn to create living characters that dance across the page, you are never lonely again. Having experienced "slumps" in my writing days, I know that loneliness can suddenly reappear. So, keep writing!

Vivian Hammond, Editor

This issue is dedicated to two young people who chose to take their own lives. Although I did not know them, I am well acquainted with the mother of Forrest, my niece, Dawna Eriksson and Jay Reed, grandmother of Mika. Jay is a long time friend and Poetry Editor of this book. My sincere condolences to you and your families.

We hope to publish annually (for now) and welcome submissions from new and experienced writers, artists and photographers. Only send copies of your work. Do not send originals (unless asked to do so). Our address is Creative Journey, 2950 White Pine Drive, Washoe Valley, NV 89704. Only submissions with a stamped return envelope will be returned. For more information send a business, stamped return envelope with your request.

To Mika

1989 - 2004

We all miss you and find you with us more than ever.

Jay Reed - Grandmother

To Forrest

1991 - 2002

For our little copperhead, achingly missed, eternally loved…Little Buggaboo, sing with the angels above… your spirit is free to find the Light… we will find you when the time is right.

Dawna Eriksson - Mother

Fiction

Poetry

The Essay

Artists

Photographers

Notes From Our Contributors

Final Pages.

Mindprint

by

Vivian Hammond

"It's never been done before," Dr. Eckwing said. He was sitting behind his desk, his elbows on the arms of his chair, letting the fingertips of his bony hands lightly touch each other. As if in prayer. James Farragut doubted, however, if the man had ever prayed in his life. Then Dr. Eckwing added, "On humans, of course." The sockets of his eyes were two black pits and the eyes even blacker. A shadow of dark hair ran from far back on his forehead to the back of his long neck. A slight look of madness, thought James. But maybe all geniuses were a little mad. At least the one before him had done marvelous things. Curing the human race of not one but two of the worst diseases of all time. One just after it had decimated half of the earth's population. The other disease, diabetes, had been a mere pittance.

James moved his long frame uneasily in the stuffed chair. "What makes you so sure it will work on my wife?"

Dr. Eckwing looked out of the second story window over the tops of the trees on the lower deck. He had a curiously gentle voice. "I'm not one hundred per cent sure. All of the experiments we have done on the lower primates have been successful as far as we can evaluate but the brain is a tricky thing. So is the mind. Your wife is basically dead. There is a body there but that's all. No thought, no movement. Just coma. We have a current mind copy on her that was done with her last physical. We know what her mind looks like from that. But her brain was seriously damaged in the accident. There is no way we can use it for a mindprint. It wouldn't work."

James looked out the windows, too. His wife, Linia, had allowed the mind copy even though it had taken hours to do. She had always been such a hypochondriac. He doubted there was a medical test in existence that she hadn't had.

James felt sweat trickle down his back under his shirt. He had lived with this horror for six months. Now there were tough decisions to be made. It was now or never.

"You have two days to make up your mind, Mr. Farragut. Then I'm afraid we will have to have some alternative solution such as releasing her to a permanent comatose hospital or letting her go. Bed space in this hospital is too scarce. I'm sorry."

Letting her go, James knew, was a nice way of saying pulling the plug. Letting her die naturally. Releasing her to a permanent comatose hospital, even if he could find space, was worse. He was broke. He had already sold the house, the car and the aircraft. The insurance liability would be gone in another week. If Linia died her life insurance would be barely enough for him to rent an apartment. At this moment he was living with Linia's mother and father. They had only tolerated him up until now. They had stopped coming to the hospital. Not being able to stand it any more. The whole thing was up to him.

"How would you get the brain?"

"There will be one available soon."

"How do you know that?"

"There will be a lethal injection given at Loralie Prison. The prisoner has signed over the rights."

"Who is it?"

"I don't think you want to know."

James leaned forward. "Why wouldn't I want to know? Is it a woman?"

"Yes, Mr. Farragut, it is a woman."

"So, you would just take out her brain and put it into Linia's skull."

Dr. Eckwing looked him in the eyes. "First we will erase the mind of the prisoner. So that it is completely clear. Then we will remove Linia's damaged brain and insert the prisoner's brain. Then we will overlay, from the mind copy we have on Linia, a mindprint into the new brain."

James thought this all sounded too easy. "That's all?"

The doctor barely smiled. "It is not as easy as it sounds. It is the most complicated surgery there is. I am the only one in the world who has ever done it."

"How can you be so sure that the prisoner's mind is completely erased?"

The doctor hesitated. "To be honest, we can't be completely sure. We are sure that the mindprint will dominate whatever traces there might be left. At least we are relatively sure of this. The mind is a delicate thing. This is still in the experimental stages. We don't know for sure what will happen."

James sat there for a moment. Trying to imagine this incredible thing being done to his wife. The woman he had slept with, ate with, gone through hell with for the past seven years. God knows he loved her. Who wouldn't? She was beautiful, yes, but there was something about her that got under his and other people's skin. Something he could never cut loose from. They had grown up together, went to school together. What would she have him do, he thought?

"I will be in touch," James said.

Before he left the hospital he went by her room. The nurses had attached automatic exercisers to her legs and lower body so that her legs were going back and forth as if she was walking even though she lay flat on her back in a coma. He thought it was a curious sight. He almost expected her to wake up so they could laugh about how silly it looked. Yet he knew it helped to keep the muscle tone.

He sat in a chair beside her bed. "I just talked to Dr. Eckwing," he said. "I have to make a decision about you in the next two days. They say you can't hear me but maybe they're wrong. You know I love you, Hon, I want to do what's best for you. Okay? I'll see you tomorrow." He stood up, leaned over and kissed her, a slow, sweet kiss. The kind he knew she really liked. He was startled when he thought, for just a second, her lips moved.

The nurse came in and turned off the machine. "Time for Beauty to rest," she said. It was Turner, the big RN with kinky red hair and enormous liquid blue eyes.

"See you tomorrow, Turner," James said.

"Okay, Handsome."

James thought that Turner looked like a fullback for the S.F. Jolts but there was something lovable about the old girl.

He was staying in the room over the garage of his in-law's home on Skywind Drive on the edge of the city. The house was slightly upper crust. At least on the outside. Inside it was somewhat confusing with furniture of every period he could imagine. His room had a bed, a tiny combo kitchen, a dresser, a TV/Video/Answering machine combination and a small bathroom with a shower. That night he looked at all the videos and telephone messages he had of Linia. Trying to get some clue about what she would do.

"Hey, Sweet Cheeks," Linia was smiling at him from the screen, "you left your socks on the floor in the bathroom again. Just to let you know, my love, they are still there and will be until the end of time until you decide to pick them up. Could you also pick up something for dinner tonight? I have two meetings today and I know I'll be dragging my tail. Can I make an appointment with you soon, Jimmie? I feel a little distance between us. You know how I hate that. Maybe in the morning? We can both be late for work. What do you say?"

Thinking back, he remembered that morning. And how she had gotten a call from her boss just as they were getting warmed up. It had put a kibosh on the whole thing.

On and on he watched. Most of it was light, nothing to base a life and death decision on. At midnight, suddenly overtaken with a piercing loneliness, he slipped on a jacket and went for a walk. A soft rain was starting to fall. He felt the world crushing down on his shoulders. About a mile from the house, down a hill onto the flat, was a large shopping center. He could see the rain misting down from the tall lights in the parking lot. The stores were mostly dark except for a small bar at the very end. Cars and bikes were parked outside and a small red sign blinked a welcome. Nighthaunt, the sign said. When he opened the thick, wooden door the throb of the old blues music and the dense, tea air surprised him a little. He had never been there. It wasn't the sort of place where he and Linia would have gone. It was small and crowded with a slight odor of unwashed humans.

He sat at the bar between a beautiful black woman and a tiny Chinese man. She had nothing on from the waist up except for gold and silver African necklaces. When she looked at him he noticed her nipples began to harden. He swallowed, raised his dark eyebrows and ordered a Nighthaunt Special from a sign he noticed above the cash register.

The drink, when it came, wasn't what he expected. At the bottom was a raw egg. Stuck on a small, red plastic pitchfork above the glass was a piece of celery, a black olive and a very slimy oyster.

"You're gonna love it," the black woman smiled.

He smiled back. Slightly repulsed, he slipped the olive and the oyster in his mouth. He had forgotten to eat dinner. Not an uncommon occurrence these days.

By two in the morning he feared raising himself off the barstool. A slight jiggle of his head brought on terrible dizziness and he had an irresistible urge to lie on the floor.

The black woman, Arla, was not in much better shape. "Come," she whispered, "I'll drive you home, Baby. You're never gonna make it up that hill."

"Okay," he slurred. "Oh, by the way, did I tell you about my wife? She's in a coma right now." He paused and looked into Arla's lonely chestnut eyes. "But she's still a very jealous woman."

Arla managed to stand up and put James' arm over her shoulder. "Oh, really. Well, I'll just mind my P's and Q's then." She laughed out loud. "You are so cute."

Outside James stepped in the biggest puddle in the parking lot. He then examined his left foot which was thoroughly soaked. Then, unsteadily they both finally got into Arla's old car.

James directed her back to his in-law's house and she drove into the driveway in front of the garage leaving the motor running and the windshield wipers working furiously. To his horror, James noticed the bedroom lights upstairs in the main house go on. A window slid open and his father-in-law's head, wild haired, stuck out.

"Go back to bed, Sabin, everything's okay." James reassured him in a loud whisper.

His father-in-law looked at them for a long moment, gave a grunt, and withdrew. The lights went off.

James decided to take the next two days off work. Designing book jackets for Liquiline Voice Books was usually a pleasure, although it didn't pay as much as he would have liked. For them to make it quite nicely, Linia more than made up the difference as a corporate tax accountant. But, of course, now she was out of the picture, so to speak, and he was on his own.

Walking barefoot along Baker Beach near the bridge, breathing the brisk air and feeling the cold foam on his feet, he was overwhelmed by the decision he must make. He kept going back to the brain, the prisoner's brain. The whole thing was such an incredible risk. He hated the idea that Linia would be a human guinea pig. But the alternatives were terrible, too. He knew she wouldn't get the care in a comatose hospital that she received now. She would waste away. Living death, he thought. And pulling the plug. That was a nightmare he wasn't sure he could deal with. And what about this prisoner? What kind of person could this be? Only mass murderers were killed these days. She must be an animal, he thought. Sitting on a large rock, he looked out at the open sea in wonder. So beautiful, so constant. Maybe if he knew more about this person the decision would be easier.

That afternoon he knocked on the door of Dr. Eckwing's laboratory in the basement of American Memorial Hospital. James had called earlier and the doctor said he would meet him there, that he was in the middle of something and couldn't leave. The doctor himself came to the door.

Birdlike in his walk, Dr. Eckwing was a good six inches taller than James and James was six feet. "Come in, Mr. Farragut, I'm sorry I couldn't see you in my office. It's important that I be here right now."

James looked around him, amazed at all the gadgets, the bottles, the cages of small animals and the one large cage where a big black animal huddled in a corner in the back. Fish swam in aquariums on one side of the room. Parts of animals or humans were in containers filled with liquid, lined up in neat rows. Some of the parts, James noticed, were brains of different sizes. The faint sweet smell of the laboratory made him nauseous.

"I wanted to talk to you about the prisoner. I want to know more about her. It's important to me. I think it will help me to make a decision."

Dr. Eckwing stared at him for a moment with his black eyes. "I see." He walked over to an examining table where a small monkey lay covered partially with a sheet. Its head was completely bandaged except for its eyes and nose. Tubes and wires were connected to it. Dr. Eckwing looked up at the monitor on the wall above it. With a finger he pushed back an eyelid and shown a light into its eye. Then he let it close again.

"Doing just fine," Dr. Eckwing whispered and stroked the tiny hand lying on its chest. "Mr. Farragut, I usually don't allow anyone in my laboratory. I've made an exception for you only because you may be part of a breakthrough never before explored by mankind. If it will help you I will see what I can do to arrange a meeting between you and the prisoner."

James was startled. He had only meant to ask a few questions. To vicariously get a feel for how the prisoner really was as a human being. But, now that this option had come up, he decided he would be a fool not to take it.

Driving through a howling rainstorm, he arrived at Loralie Prison several miles away in the country at ten the next morning. Pacing back and forth in the waiting area, he became aware that cameras placed in various parts of the room, moved with him. It gave him an uncomfortable, yet secure, feeling knowing that his every move was being watched.

When she came in with the guard, he was shocked. She wasn't at all what he expected. Looking more like she had come from a convent than death row. She was slight, with thin brown hair and pale skin. Dressed in a simple cotton dress.

"Hello," he said, nervously, "I'm James Farragut."
She stared at him coldly. "Tonia Ross. You're her husband?"
"Yes."

"What do you want?" Her voice had a cruel tone in it. "You will have my brain, what more do you want?"

"I just wanted to meet you. To talk to you." He sat down in a chair by a table and put his head in his hands. Suddenly feeling terrible about being there. "I'm sorry, I don't really know why I'm here. I'm trying to make a choice about my wife. Whether to pull the plug and let her die or let them do this surgery. I know you must have too much on your mind to be talking to me. I shouldn't have come." He got up and looked at the guard standing by the door. As if to conclude the meeting.

"No wait," Tonia said, "don't go. Please, don't go."

They both sat down at the table, taking each other in.

She gave him a faint smile. "It's just that I've been under a strain lately."

He smiled back. "I can imagine."

"My lawyers keep promising they're going to get me out of this. I try to keep believing them. I don't want to know that they're all full of shit. Even though they are."

James' voice broke. "It must be terrible." He had never been with someone who was facing certain death in the next few days. He always lived with the optimism that he and everyone he knew would at least live to be a hundred, the new median age in the last census.

"I didn't kill all those people. I have a hard time killing the cockroaches in my cell. There was a bloody massacre. I fainted when it all started. When I woke up I had the weapon in my hands. My fingerprints were all over. There were two young men, half naked, leather and spikes. They broke in while we were having a party. We were snorting to beat the band. One of them grabbed me and said they would kill me if the rest of them didn't give them all their money and drugs. That's when I fainted. When I woke up there was blood and bodies everywhere. That's when the cops came."

She had misty green eyes that seemed to search his face. Her hands were quietly locked together in front of her on the table. For a moment, when he looked at the long tapering fingers, it was almost like seeing Linia's.

"Don't worry about my brain. I've done a little drugs but not much. I hope the surgery works so that you and your wife can get on with your life if that's the way you choose. In a small way, I guess I will go on living, too." She smiled at him. "You remind me of my ex. He had black hair and blue eyes like you. But you're much prettier. I'll be thinking about you, Sugar."

When James left the prison he realized he was leaving with a feeling that Tonia was okay. Although he didn't know whether to believe her about her guilt or innocence, she had not been the awful person he had imagined she would be.

Back in the room over the garage he got out all the cards, letters and notes that Linia had given him over the years. Still trying to find something that would give him an inkling about what she herself would do. How she would deal with all of this if it had been him that had gotten into that terrible accident on the freeway that morning. Then he found it. Handwritten words at the bottom of a small poem in an anniversary card she had given him a few months before. "I want to be with you forever, my Darling, when we are both old and white-haired I want to be by your side. I love you always, Linia." It choked him up then and it was choking him up now.

His decision made, he again knocked on the door of Dr. Eckwing's laboratory. The doctor calmly accepted his decision. "The surgery will be done Friday morning right after the lethal injection at the prison. It will be a very long surgery. All day and part of the night. So don't get worried." He was busy doing things while he talked. The monkey that he was attending to the day before was awake and moving in a nearby cage. The big black thing in the large cage turned out to be a young gorilla who watched James curiously. "This is Saidie," Dr. Eckwing said. "She's very sweet." The gorilla stuck her hand out of her cage as if to touch Dr. Eckwing. The doctor took the hand gently and shook it. Saidie took hold of his hand, much to James' astonishment, and held it to her chest. She then began to lick it affectionately. Then she let it go and went back in her corner to watch them both. James smiled with relief.

Friday came with startling suddenness. He had not slept. He could barely eat. Most of his time was spent in the chair next to Linia's bed. Until Turner kicked him out.

"For God's sake, Handsome, go somewhere for awhile. Get

something to eat. Get some sleep. Leave us alone so I can get Beauty ready for all this."

And so he left. And wandered around. He went into the Nighthaunt and spent hours with Arla having one Nighthaunt Special after another. She practically carried him out to her car. His in-laws barely spoke to him. He told them of his decision. They both cried and he cried, too. What else could he do?

"We know you love our daughter, James. We know it's been hard." Sabin was a big, clean-cut man with a bulging abdomen. A very successful real estate manager.

His small, blond mother-in-law, Lila Marie, gave him a long hug. "Try not to drink so much, James. It's not good for you."

Red-eyed and hung over, he nodded obediently. "I know."

Friday morning at dawn he was in her room to look at her once more before they took her to surgery. Turner was there. She had shaved off Linia's long yellow hair and bathed her head in some orangish liquid. He gave Linia a slow, sweet kiss. "I'll be just outside, Hon. I'll be waiting. Okay?"

Turner gave him a tender smile. "She's a lucky woman to have a guy like you."

He swallowed hard. "Thanks, Turner."

It was easily the longest day of his life. He paced. He read. He went into the cafeteria and tried to eat. His in-laws came in, sat and stared. At ten o'clock that night, the door to the operating section swung open and nurses and doctors flooded through it. Dr. Eckwing came up to him.

"She's in recovery. You can go in for a few minutes but that's all. She's still very drowsy."

James looked into the doctor's tired face. "Well, how was it? Did it go okay?"

"The surgery itself went fine. We will know better in the morning if everything is working the way it should."

James was so relieved he could have cried. Quietly, he went into her room. Her face looked serene, as always. Her head was bandaged so that only part of her face showed through. He sat in a chair and kissed her hand. "I'm right here, Hon. You're going to be okay. I know you're going to be okay."

Linia slept on soundly.

A few minutes later a nurse came through the door. "I'm sorry, Mr. Farragut, you'll have to leave now."

He spent the rest of the night in the waiting room down the hall. Scrunched down in the leather couch, sleeping fitfully. Other people came and went but he stayed. Morning finally broke through the tall windows and he blinked at it. A nurse came in and tossed the morning paper on the coffee table. Smiling at him. Politely, he smiled back. He took the paper and went into the cafeteria ordering a large coffee.

At first the headlines didn't register. Then they hit like a club. No, how could this be? He ran to Dr. Eckwing's office but it was early, about six thirty. He ran back to Linia's room. Empty.

Two nurses were bent over a console at the nurse's station. "Where's my wife, Linia Farragut?"

The tall, dark haired nurse looked up. "She's been moved, Mr. Farragut. She can't have visitors right now. She's in room 021 downstairs in the basement. You will have to talk to Dr. Eckwing. I'm sorry."

Of course, he thought. The doctor wanted her to be near his laboratory so that he could attend to her personally. But something had gone wrong. Very wrong.

He knocked on the laboratory door. Dr. Eckwing opened it sleepily. "Yes."

"I want to know what happened," James was in a frenzy. "You tell me what happened, doctor. What did you do to my wife?"

The doctor stared at him quietly. "Mr. Farragut, I had to make some hard choices. I did not anticipate the prisoner having a stay of execution. How was I to know someone would come out of the woodwork and confess to the crime she was accused of ? I had to use another brain. I had no choice. Now, go away. I'm very tired."

"Whose brain? What happened?"

"We'll talk in another hour. Come back then."

"I want to see my wife."

Dr. Eckwing pointed to a room opposite his own. Room 021. Quietly, James went in. A nurse sat in a chair in a corner dozing. She opened her eyes and looked up at him.

"The doctor said I could see my wife," he whispered. She got up to leave. "Where's Turner? She's my wife's private nurse."

"I don't know. I was given this assignment yesterday."

James frowned.

The nurse smiled. "I'll be right outside."

For the first time in six months, Linia opened her eyes. He stared at her with such joy he thought he would burst. That old look of love was written on her beautiful features.

"James, Honey," she whispered.

Tears of joy ran down his face. "I've waited for you, Lin."

On and on they talked. How, he thought, could he have ever doubted Dr. Eckwing. He was a genius. He had done the impossible. His Linia was back. Back to stay. And Tonia had escaped the lethal injection. He could only thank God for such a wonderful day. At last his life could continue. The sun had finally broken through the awful clouds of despair.

The hour passed. "I have to go talk to the doctor, Hon. You just rest now. Okay? I'll be back soon."

She smiled at him tenderly and held out her hand. He took it and kissed it. "I love you so much, Linia."

"I love you, too, James." Slowly and gently she held his hand to her breast and, to his astonishment, began to lick his fingers.

His heart began to pound. He jerked back his hand. "Why did you do that? Why did you lick my hand?"

She searched his face. "I don't know."

Backing out of the room, he stumbled out the door. The nurse stared at him for a moment then went back into the room.

James burst through the laboratory door. Dr. Eckwing lay on a cot on the other side of the room, jerking himself up at the noise James had made. James ran to the gorilla cage. A great mound lay on the floor covered with a bloody sheet. His emotions went wild. "What did you do, you maniac? What did you do?"

Dr. Eckwing held his head in his hands. "I saved your wife's life, Mr. Farragut. I sacrificed someone else's for her."

"You gave her a gorilla brain?"

"Yes, but the mindprint took well. I tested it thoroughly. Only tiny traces were left of the gorilla mind. No one will know except you and I."

James stared at him in disbelief. Trying to digest this amazing thing that had happened. "She licked my hand."

Dr. Eckwing nodded. "Saidie was a sweet animal."

"So, what else will she do?"

"I don't know. We'll just have to see."

When James went back into Room 021, he stared at Linia for a long time. She slept serenely. A soft smile on her beautiful lips. He was exhausted. He lay his head down on the edge of the bed and closed his eyes. He wondered what the future held. Wondered what else was in store now that Linia had Saidie's brain. She had licked his hand, a gentle sweet thing to do. Something a sweet, young gorilla had done. Yet when he looked into Linia's face and saw that old look of complete love, he knew it was really Linia in there. If Saidie occasionally showed herself by licking his hand or swinging from the chandelier, he didn't care. Linia had opened her eyes again. They could go on now.

###

Healing One Spirit At A Time

by

Kim Henrick

The little horse's coat was a wonderful mix of colors - like a dessert of vanilla and chocolate ice cream topped off with a black-licorice mane. Unfortunately, his beauty could not help him with his present predicament; the colt had a serious leg injury and he would not survive the winter without help. He needed humans, a hospital and money, things not afforded wild horses in the harsh Nevada desert.

The four month old colt was observed struggling to keep up with his mother and their wild horse band on private land near Stagecoach, Nevada on October 7, 1998. After six days, a Nevada brand inspector finally trapped him and took the colt to be examined by the state's veterinarian. The diagnosis and prognosis were grim: the colt had a broken leg and the State of Nevada wasn't about to fix it.

The brand inspector phoned Wild Horse Spirit (WHS), a wild horse sanctuary in Washoe Valley, Nevada, south of Reno. Bobbi Royle listened silently to the sad story and, as usual, without hesitation, accepted full responsibility for the injured horse. Bobbi and WHS co-founder, Betty Kelly, named the little horse "Spirit" and then embarked on a rescue effort that would truly test their dedication to these wild creatures.

X-rays revealed a fracture high in Spirit's left front leg near the point of his elbow. A metal plate needed to be installed to fixate the fracture but the surgery couldn't be done in Reno. The closest place with adequate facilities and expertise was the prestigious (and very expensive) Veterinary Teaching Hospital at the University of California at Davis

"Spirit" with Betty Kelly (left) and Bobbi Royle (behind) at Wild Horse Spirit - 10/4 - © 2004 Kim Henrick

"Spirit" on left at Wild Horse Spirit - 10/4 - © 2004 Kim Henrick

I asked Bobbi and Betty if they ever consider the consequences of helping a horse in need.

"No, we don't, we can't, we just do what we have to do."

(U.C. Davis), near Sacramento. It would be a hard trip over the Sierra Nevada for the injured horse but Spirit was going to U.C. Davis - it was his only hope for survival.

At the hospital, as if choreographed, the precision team of doctors and interns moved purposefully around in their blue scrubs and grubby athletic shoes. With specific, prearranged duties they examined Spirit, calmed him, tended to some lacerations, and implanted the metal plate. The surgery was a great success. Then began the long recovery stage.

Back home in Washoe Valley and confined to twelve-foot stalls for the next five months, the bored colt played with toys, studied his new horse and human friends, and enjoyed his catered meals. In early March 1999, Spirit was hauled off again to U.C. Davis to have the plate removed. Later that same month, among his friends at WHS, it was time to take Spirit out for a test drive. As Betty and Bobbi covered their eyes, and Spirit's new wild horse friends looked on with interest, Spirit raced at full speed toward the fence at the opposite side of the large arena. Just before crashing into the fence he dug his hooves into the dirt and jarred to a stop. Finally, after what seemed like minutes, the dust settled and Spirit pranced away without a limp. Spirit's rescuers had waited five long months and spent nearly $6,000 to be frightened like that. In fact, Betty, a retired pediatrician, and Bobbi, a retired engineer, had long ago traded well-deserved, easy-chair retirements for just such an occasional reward.

Spirit is one of more than one hundred wild horses that WHS has helped in some fashion since 1989. The help comes in many forms: **feeding the horses when their grazing areas have been bulldozed into sub-divisions, patching up a horse after an all-too-frequent car accident, transplanting a wild horse to a safe refuge, monitoring mustanger activity and legislative efforts and facilitating some high-standard adoption processes.**

WHS became a federal (501) (c) (3) charitable organization in 1993 and in 2000 was granted Sanctuary status (bestowed by the Association of Sanctuaries). To say that WHS is a "non-profit" is a gross understatement, yet somehow it succeeds with bake sales, garage sales, generous donations, plenty of hard work and strong borrowed backs.

Spirit is full grown now. He's muscular and lean and sports a glistening long black mane and a silky white tail that reaches nearly to the ground. While we watched this beautiful horse play with his friends recently, I asked Bobbi and Betty if they ever consider the consequences of helping a wild horse in need. They shook their heads back and forth. Betty added, "No, we don't, we can't, we just do what we have to do." With that, they turned and headed out again to tend to another spirit in need.

                                                                    ###

To help Wild Horse Spirit or to find out more about wild horses, please visit their website at: www.wildhorsespirit.org or call 883-5488.

Letters From Jeb

by

Vivian Hammond

The first curious letter came one early December morning just before Christmas. It was among Christmas cards, bills and sales papers in a plain white envelope. It caught her eye because her name, Willa, was only spelled with one L.

"Dear Wila," it began, "I thought I would write and inquire as to your health and was wondering if California was all I've heard about. Is it true that it never gets cold there?" The handwriting was in black ink, plain, almost childlike. She read it on the BART train to San Francisco. On vacation from her job, she was going into the city to do the last of her Christmas shopping hoping to get everything wrapped and under the tree so that she could have a few days of sanity before the big day.

The postmark was Holdenville, Oklahoma, the little town where she was born. She didn't know anyone there. Hadn't for years. She read the letter three times trying to make sense out of it. It spoke of her grandfather, William Stiles, and how he was going to build another room onto the little house where he and Grandma lived. "If the Lord was willing," the letter said. It talked of the heavy snows they had been having and how some of the kids had been sick. One of the horses, Clover, had fallen through the ice in a deep pond and was killed. "Dadgum dogs were chasing her." It closed by saying he hoped everything was fine with her family and her in California and the letter was signed, Jeb.

She stared out the rain-flecked window of the train watching the emerald countryside of Lafayette and Orinda pass by. Wondering about the letter. Her grandfather and grandmother had been dead for over forty years. And she knew no one named Jeb.

Christmas came and went as always with the grand crescendo occurring Christmas morning when her two sons and their families descended upon the house for breakfast and gift opening. Try as she might, even though weeks passed, she could not get the letter out of her mind. When she read it she felt as if she was in a time warp of some kind. If someone was playing a joke, it wasn't funny.

It was in the middle of May when her job was going full tilt that the second letter came. She was in the midst of preparing a major presentation for her part of the design of a large computerized system for her company. Her mind felt like it was in shreds. Her energy level felt as if she had been out rock climbing which she liked to do now and then. To prove something to herself. She wasn't sure what but something. As before the letter came in a small, white envelope written in black ink with her name again spelled with one L. It had much the same flavor as the other except that this time the letter mentioned the war and how it had effected Red. How he was much more silent than he had ever been. "Sometimes he just stares," it said. "Mr. and Mrs. Stiles are both well. Mr. Stiles is fixin' to start on the room come the thaw." It ended as before hoping that her family was well in California. "Is it a fact that it's always warm there? And, by the way, do you still have that mark on your right arm?" Then it was signed, Jeb.

She was sitting at her desk in front of her computer. She looked at the mark on top of her right forearm. A birthmark the size of a half dollar about four inches up from her wrist. How could he know that?

The return address was General Delivery, Holdenville, Oklahoma with no zip code. She read the letter again. Wondering what kind of hoax was being played on her. What bothered her was that it sounded real. So incredibly real.

She remembered having an uncle named Red who had died several years ago. She had known him when she was a child. He was a tall, sweet man with dark auburn hair who had led a short, unhappy life. She remembered how his nose would crinkle up when he laughed. And how she had liked him. Strange how this Jeb knew her family.

On her lunch hour she called her mother in Nevada hoping to shed some light on what was going on.

"Well," her mother said slowly, "I do seem to remember a Jeb." She spoke hesitantly, which was unlike her. "Why do you want to know?" Her mother could always tell when something was up. She had a peculiar radar that had always forced Willa to tell the truth even when it would have been best to skirt it.

"I know it's weird, Mom, but I've gotten a couple of letters from Holdenville, Oklahoma from someone named Jeb. He seems to know the family very well. He seems to know me." She didn't want to go into detail. It was all too strange. The way the letters were written. As if everyone was still alive. Living their lives in the fashion they would have then.

"If you really want to know, Willa, I'll call Lola. She started a family tree a few years back."

Lola was Willa's aunt, her mother's sister, who lived in southern California with her daughter, Lenore.

"Are you writing back?"

Willa hesitated. It hadn't occurred to her to write back. It would almost seem like she would be going along with everything. But still, maybe her mother had a point. It could be a way of finding out what was really happening.

"No, I haven't yet. But maybe I will."

"I'll let you know what Lola says. How are you otherwise? Did you go to the doctor about those headaches?" Willa's mother could gently push her to take care of herself in spite of her own disinterest.

"Not yet."

"When?"

"Soon."

Her presentation to other meaningful members of the project uncovered embarassing flaws in her work. She would have to go back to the users, get better documentation, draw more diagrams and hold another meeting. People who had other pieces of the project, which were based on hers, were waiting for her. She had mental images of them drumming their fingers on their desks looking toward her cubicle. Which probably wasn't far from the truth. She was now past her deadline. The pressure cooker was boiling. After work she changed into a jogging suit, hit the path around the building and grounds, visited a snack machine, came back to her desk and went back to work. At midnight, she left. In slightly better shape than when the meeting adjourned. At least, she thought, I didn't panic. Not yet.

Her mother, who normally went to bed with the chickens, called her at eleven the following night. Willa had just gotten home from work.

"No wonder you have headaches. Working until all hours."

"Sometimes I have to, Mom. Deadlines."

"Well, just don't kill yourself. No job is worth it."

"I know. So, are you okay? Isn't it a little past your bed time?"

"Yes, but I thought you'd like to know what Lola said."

Willa sat down at the kitchen table and grabbed a pen and tablet out of her briefcase. She was thinking she might be drawing a family tree.

"Guess what?"

Willa laughed. "What?"

"There were two Jebs. Distant cousins. Years and years ago. One lived to be eighty two and the other only seventeen. Does he sound old or young?"

"I can't tell. Tell me more."

"Old Jeb was born and died in Holdenville. He disappeared a couple of years ago. They think he wandered off and fell in a hole or drowned or something. They're pretty sure he's gone."

Willa, for some reason, felt bad at this news even though he was a stranger to her. The letters had caused a vague bonding with this Jeb person. He was so innocent sounding. His question about California, was it always warm, had been part of a myth she had heard before that people in the old days had believed. The land of sunshine. The land of milk and honey. They truly believed that it never got cold in California. It was almost childlike. Touching somehow.

"What about young Jeb?"

Her mother drew a breath. "Well, he's kind of interesting. He once lived down the road from my mother and father. Third or fourth cousin. Do you want a copy of the whole thing? She has clippings from the local newspaper on many of the births and deaths. Sounds really interesting."

"Sure, why not."

Months passed before the third letter came. Her piece of the project had long ago been blessed by her counterparts and was headfirst into a later stage of it. Going through the same anxiety as she had before. Such was the life of a design specialist, she kept telling herself.

Jeb, as always, was friendly. He discussed the coming fall. Then the tone of the letter changed. He wondered what she thought about how the war had ended. "I stayed up all night when I heard," he said. "I couldn't believe my country would do a thing like that. I know Roosevelt wouldn't have done it."

She frowned when she read the letter. Then tears came into her eyes. She realized that he was talking about the dropping of atomic bombs on the Japanese ending World War II. The way he made it sound it seemed like only yesterday. Like Jeb, she couldn't sleep that night. The horror of that incident was so fresh she could almost hear the screams. She must write back.

She must find out who Jeb really was. Could the old man who had supposedly disappeared reappeared? Was he living in an old folks home somewhere so senile that no one was paying attention that he was sending out letters that were upsetting her life? He ended the letter by saying, "Sure hope to see you at the family reunion on September 15th. I'm looking forward to it. I get to make the ice cream this time. I miss you so, Wila. We had such good times before you went away."

His words touched her deeply. How could she have ever forgotten someone like Jeb.

Unsteadily, she began the letter. She felt as if she were writing to a ghost.

"Dear Jeb," she began, "thank you for your letters. I hope you are well. I'm sorry to say that it does get very cold at times in California although I'm sure the weather is very mild compared to Oklahoma." She stopped. Unable to continue. This was crazy, she thought. How could she go along with this hoax even if it did sound real? It was like she was getting sucked into the whole lie. She wouldn't do it.

The package containing the family tree came on a Saturday about two weeks after Jeb's letter. Willa was in her front yard pulling weeds around her roses when it came. The brisk-walking mailman, young and dark, handed it to her.

When she looked at the large envelope she got the same feeling that she had when she received Jeb's letters. Her name, Willa, printed in black on the package, was spelled with one L.

"How strange," she said out loud.

"Excuse me?" Said the mailman.

"Oh, it's nothing. Thanks." Immediately she took the package inside and began pouring over it. Her Aunt Lola was a meticulous woman. Each name was spelled out in full. Addresses below them with dates signifying current or last known address. Dates of births and deaths. Even pictures. There was a note on top from her aunt.

"Dear Wila," it said, "sorry for the delay in mailing this. I've been pretty sick but am feeling much better. You can keep the package if you want to carry it on. I got tired of doing it. My rheumatism and all. If you don't want to, you can send it back. Sending love to all, Aunt Lola."

Willa stared at the note. Puzzling over her Aunt Lola's spelling of Willa. She wondered if there could be a connection somehow. Maybe her aunt was not as meticulous as she first thought.

There were dozens of pictures, old black and whites. Queer pictures, some of them of stone-faced men and women in front of old cars and buildings. No pretend smiles in Kodacolor, she thought. Children, too, often stairsteps of each other, and the women who had them year after year and the tired looking men who struggled to feed them. She turned a few of them over and found names printed neatly on the back. Gradually, after looking into their faces for a long time, they began to lose their strangeness. They were her ancestors from another time with hopes, dreams and failures just like her. Most of them had already lived their lives. She began, in a mysterious way, to love them.

She read some of the newspaper clippings. Strictly small town stuff, she thought. But as she read she became more and more intrigued. Much of it was from another era, a time gone by. Many were written as if the editor was part of the family, affectionately, from the inside. The last clipping was one describing a family reunion. Quickly, she read it. Yes, she thought, it was the one on September 15th. "It started out to be a fine affair," it said," but tragedy hit hard. The Stiles family lost one of its own that dark day."

Willa's eyes widened. "Oh God, I can't believe this."

She stared at the calendar on the kitchen wall above the stove. September 1. The words in the article shocked her. "Young Jeb Stiles died suddenly, choking on a piece of steak."

She was stunned. It was more like a future prediction than the reporting of something that happened over forty years ago. On and on she read, trying to piece her family tree together. She found her mother and father, her four brothers and herself. She glanced at her name printed carefully under her brother John's. It was spelled Willa. Then she searched for the two Jebs. Names, addresses, birth dates, dates of death, references to news articles and histories. It was a remarkable work of research. Page after page. How could there be a connection between herself and this Jeb. It didn't make sense. Nothing made sense. At last she found Jeb Stiles, Jebediah Graham Stiles, born 1905, disappeared 1987. Children, Ora, Mary, Jebediah and Wila.

Willa stared at the children's names, Jebediah and Wila. There was the connection, sister and brother. Wila Stiles, born January 8, 1937. Funny, she thought, it was her own birth date. Now she felt certain that the letters had to have been written to Jeb's sister because of Jeb signing his first name rather than Father or Dad to indicate the older Jeb.

It was all so strange and confusing. The past was somehow getting mixed up with the future. She was in the middle of it for no reason. Who was this Wila, Jeb's sister? She went back to her own name. Born January 8, 1937.

She had spread the package over her kitchen table by the tall windows. She looked out at the cool shadows on her patio mixing with brilliant sunlight.

The small tree growing in her brick flowerbed had strewn pale yellow leaves on the stone. She got up and wandered around her big house. The drapes were open letting in the light, illuminating the old furniture and various pictures and paintings she had placed here and there. She wanted to talk to someone, anyone, yet she hesitated. They would think she was crazy. She stared into the mirror of her dresser. A tall, handsome, dark-haired woman stared back. Maybe she lived alone too long. Letting her imagination play with the letter and the family tree. Maybe she was a little crazy.

It was September 1. Fourteen days before the supposed family reunion. Why did she feel panic? Something that happened over forty years ago had nothing to do with here and now. She sat on her bed and held her head in her hands. Or did it?

On Monday she called Holdenville, Oklahoma information. She

asked for a records clerk for births and deaths. They referred her to a county clerk. She was on the phone for quite awhile. She could feel the slowed pace even over the phone. It was as if everything had shifted into low gear. Maybe, she thought, that's really how it should be instead of the running pace of San Francisco. The fast track. She would have to write to Oklahoma City, send a fee, give dates, then they would send a copy of birth certificates, hers and this other Wila's. There was no time for all this. She hung up the phone.

She called the Holdenville newspaper, the Holdenville Express. They kept track of births and deaths. One of the few professional things they seemed to do.

"Yes, we print them all," the voice said on the phone. It was a man's voice, deep and drawled. She found it pleasant. Many of her older relatives sounded much the same. "I guess I could look something up for you."

She told him what she wanted. Was there a Wila Stiles and a Willa James born on January 8, 1937 in Holdenville? It was a weekly newspaper she found out and sometimes a week got skipped. If he was sick or went on vacation, he said. She smiled when he said that. It was obvious he was not from the hard driving school of journalism.

"Call me after lunch," the voice said.

"Thanks, I really appreciate this."

"It's all right. You sound like a nice lady. Have you been back here lately?"

"No, I left when I was a baby."

"Oh, are you one of these Willa's?"

"Yes, I am."

"Okay, Willa, call me back. My name's Kent Dale."

"Okay, thanks Kent Dale."

After lunch, about two, she called him.

"Just one Willa born in Holdenville on January 8, 1937. Mother is Mary and father is Jebediah Stiles. Sorry to say the mother died in childbirth. Very sad story, Willa."

When she hung up she had an empty feeling inside. Her piece of the puzzle was missing. Something wasn't right. She called her Aunt Lola.

"Well, I'll be darned," her Aunt Lola said, "Lenore, guess who's on the phone. It's your cousin, Wila."

Willa explained that there was only one Willa of record born on that day in Holdenville. Her Aunt Lola hesitated. There was something reluctant in her speech. "Well, maybe you need to talk to your mother, Wila. She would know more than me."

That night she called her mother. "Willa, I'm coming down there this weekend. We can talk about it then."

"Mom, why can't we talk about it now?"

"It's kind of complicated, Honey. I'll see you Friday evening about seven if the traffic isn't too bad."

Time was going by. The days were slipping away. September 15th would be here soon.

When her mother arrived on Friday, she put her off even more. "Let's go out to dinner. Somewhere quiet."

Willa laughed. "Mom, are you avoiding talking to me about this or what?"

She looked into her mother's faded brown eyes. They had never had secrets before.

"At dinner, Willa. Okay? I need to eat and relax. I've been very tense lately."

Willa picked a steak house out on the highway. It had individual tables enclosed partially with darkened glass partitions. Sort of open privacy, she thought.

After they ordered Willa waited for her mother to begin. For the first time in her life she realized that her mother found it difficult to look her in the eye.

"Mom, is there something wrong?"

"Willa," she said finally, "I knew Mary and Jeb Stiles."

Willa's eyes widened. "You did?"

"Jeb was my cousin. We played together as children. Went to school together. He was my close friend as well. We were sort of kissin' cousins although we never kissed, of course. He married one of my friends, Mary Radcliff."

Willa listened, fascinated. Her mother seldom talked of her childhood.

"When she died he went crazy. It was like his world had come to an end. And there he was with all those kids and a new baby to boot."

Willa stared at her mother, suddenly comprehending the whole situation. A sharp realization hit her hard. A question loomed high in her mind nearly lodging in her throat.

"Was I that baby?"

The woman across from her, looking small and vulnerable in the soft candlelight, dissolved into tears. The sweet, warm mother that had been a rock in her life. Nothing is as it seems, she thought. My mother is not my mother. My father, my brothers. What else is a lie? And what else is the truth? The birth dates for Wila and Willa had turned out to be true.

"I tried to tell you a million times. Jeb promised not to get in touch with you but maybe he couldn't keep still any more. I thought he had died. I thought the secret died, too. I'm sorry, Willa. I didn't want to deceive you. You are my daughter. You didn't come out of my body but you are still my daughter."

Willa became so confused and bewildered she began to cry. Silently, they ate dinner. The connection between them, so strong all her life, was broken. Willa never experienced such emptiness. What about her real family, she thought? What about Jeb?

After her mother went to bed that night Willa got out the family tree package. She went back over each picture carefully. There were dozens, all different sizes. Then she found what she was looking for. A small picture with a tall, moustached man in a crumpled hat and four children. A shaggy haired boy with big eyes was looking solemnly into the camera. He was holding a tiny baby close to his chest. On the back it listed their names, Jeb Stiles and children, Ora, Mary, little Jeb and baby Wila. Her other family.

Lovingly, she touched Jeb's face with her fingers.

When she woke the next morning her mother had gone. A note lay on the kitchen table. "Dear Willa, please forgive me for not telling you. I will always love you. Mother."

It was September 6th. Why did she feel this panic? September 15th was coming, the day of the reunion. Now she had to write the letter. She must. Something inside her told her to warn him. Let him know he would die this day. She could not go to work. She felt consumed. Perhaps she should go to Holdenville. See for herself. Know what a terrible lie this all was. This awful trick someone was playing. Yet there was truth mixed in with the lie. He knew so much about her. He knew about the mark on her arm.

She wrote the letter in a frenzy. It had to be written and sent today to make sure he didn't go to the reunion. "Trust me, Jeb, my friend, my brother, DO NOT GO TO THE REUNION. Something terrible will happen to you. Please, please, I beg you, do not go."

She rushed to the post office and mailed it. Some of the panic softened. At least now he had a chance.

She went to work the next day. She was between assignments but was still needed for her input in meetings and advice and counsel for field representatives. Her knowledge, having grown with the building of the computer system, was extensive.

At midnight on September 8th the telephone beside her bed began to ring. She turned on the small lamp on her night table and picked it up.

"Hello."

At first there was silence. Then she heard the soft crying, sobbing of a woman. "Mom, is that you?"

Then the telephone went dead, a dial tone.

She called her mother instantly. How could she have hurt her this way? The woman who had raised her and loved her all her life.

On the third ring her mother answered. By her voice, Willa knew she had woke her. "Willa, what's wrong? Why are you calling me at this hour?"

Willa bit her lip. She had not talked to her mother since that night at the restaurant. "I'm sorry, Mom. I just called to tell you how much I love you."

For a few minutes they talked. Rebuilding their connection to each other between tears and laughter.

"Everybody always says I look exactly like you," Willa laughed. "What do you think when they say that?"

"Well, I look a lot like your real mother. A little better looking, though. No, I'm just kidding. She was a fine looking woman."

When they finally hung up Willa lay in her bed in the dark watching the slender tree outside her window moving gently in the night wind. She wondered about the crying woman. Relieved it hadn't been her mother.

The next day she called Kent Dale in Holdenville. Could he give her any information about Jeb Stiles?

As before he asked her to call back in the afternoon.

"I'm putting her to bed today so things are pretty hectic." She knew he meant he was printing the paper today. One of the few things she had learned in journalism class.

"I have a couple of little things on young Jeb," Kent Dale said when she called him. "School stuff mostly. Nice young fellow, it looks like. I'll send copies."

"Thanks Kent Dale. I really appreciate this."

"No problem. By the way, are you going to the reunion?"

Willa was stunned. "Reunion?"

"Yes, I have it right here. September 15th in the park. The whole Stiles clan will be there. At least most of it, I guess."

"I don't know."

When she hung up she was flabberghasted. "I can't believe this!" She found she was shouting at the walls in her house. "What is going on? Am I going crazy?"

She booked a flight to Oklahoma City for September 14th. She had to know if she was losing her mind or if this insanity could be uncovered there. She would rent a car at the airport and drive to the little town to the park. She would see these people. This family so far away. She would watch for Jeb. She would look into his eyes and know him. He would not die this day. She would not let him.

On the night of the twelfth she lay in her bed in the darkness. She slept deeply letting her dreams wander in her mind. The distant ringing of a telephone broke through her haze. She turned over and switched on the light.

"Hello."

Again the silence, then the quiet sobbing of a woman.

"Wait, don't hang up. Please, who are you? What do you want from me? Don't cry now. Please, don't hang up."

Slowly the crying began to subside. "Wila."

The sound of her own name shocked her. "Yes, this is Willa. Who are you?"

"This is Mary. Mary Stiles, your sister. I know you don't know me. I tried to talk to you the other night but I lost my nerve."

Willa drew a breath, feeling her emotions pump through her body. All those wasted years, she thought.

"It's so good to hear your voice, Mary. I'm sorry I never knew you."

"I'm sorry, too. We all knew you, though. You were our little baby doll. We saw pictures of you as you were growing up that your mother sent to her mother here. Jeb loved you so. Played with you all the time before they took you. He wrote dozens of letters to you that he could never send. He was a sweet gentle boy. When he died I had all of his things. All of his letters to you, signed and sealed." She began to cry again. And Willa began to cry, too. It was too late. Her brother Jeb was really gone. "Every year I get the blues thinking about him especially around reunion time. I wanted you to have those letters the way he would have sent them to you. I'm so sorry, Wila, I never realized how it would affect you. When I got the mail the other day your letter to Jeb was in it. I felt so bad about it. You were so frightened for him."

The next morning Willa sat at her kitchen table staring out at her patio and yard. The shadows and sunlight, the dark green grass, the stone patio strewn with yellow leaves. All she could think about was Mary Stiles and Jeb. The sudden turn of her life.

At last she lifted the receiver of her telephone and called her mother.

"Mom, I'm going to a family reunion in Holdenville. Would you like to go with me?"

The soft, loving voice. "Yes, I would love to."

The End

To my mother.

HOW A POEM HAPPENS

When I was asked to write about my "personal approach to poetry", I must admit I was at a loss. This was not something that had ever consciously entered my mind. I don't think I've ever deliberately sat down to compose a poem, and it seemed a bit intimidating to try to describe how it comes about.

For me, a poem has a life of its own. It starts with a whiff of melody, a memory, a few words that start tugging at the edge of awareness, or an impression of an incident that refuses to be forgotten.

It starts like a seed or bulb underground, unseen but working its way toward the surface until it breaks through and can no longer be ignored. When I have the germ of the idea, I start to play with it until it takes shape, altering words as they seem imperative or appropriate.

Sitting at the keyboard, I let the ideas give birth to the words that will shape them. Putting it all down as the spirit moves me, I change a word or line here and there until I think it's the best I can do at the moment. Then I let the completed poem hover in place until a bit of time passes. Upon reading the new creation, I may see an expression or phrase that should be changed to improve the whole. Then I retype the finished entity, and from then on, the poem is on its own. Giving birth is often a struggle, but sometimes worth the labor pains.

As I was trying to find a way to describe how a poem comes about, I happened to read a magazine article about a 94-year-old painter and poet who was asked how she wrote her poems. She replied, "Well, sometimes an idea keeps rolling around in your head, or a pair of words, but you don't really know what it is. It has to *emerge.*" For her, a couple of words seen on a roadside took fifty years to become a poem. Fortunately, I have had hundreds of poems break through the surface and come to light, however that happens. It's only *my* way, not really a choice or a recipe for other poets.

Jay Reed - 5/1/04

LEAFING, LEAVING

All summer garbed in serious young green

vines and trees labor silently

infusing their precious fruit

with sweet substance to share.

Harvest past, spent leaves

enter their mid-life turning

maples rewarding even the undeserving

fling down a shower of golden stars.

But with the sap retreating

a flame is kindled everywhere

searing slivers of pistachio & blazing liquidambar

crimson smokeless fires in riotous vineyard rows.

Trees so red they seize our sight

autumn burnished full of brightness signaling

this time of endings - a glorious goodbye

rustling scarlet banners wave in leaving.

BEAUTIFUL FRAGRANCE

The end of May with everything in bloom

old trees and greenery cluster around the grass

in that sheltered garden, beloved retreat

leaves fluttering at your sudden flight.

Now you are borne on the breeze like the essence of

lilacs

everywhere we turn you perfume the late spring air.

Like a rash fledgling launched from the bough

risking everything, even your unspread wings

leaving us earthbound who would have tried

to mend what was broken

to drive off the demons

to dry the stifled tears hidden in your darkness

Mika: "beautiful fragrance"

forgive us our blindness

our powerless love.

LEARN TO BE FREE
By Mika Drew

Learn to be free.

Run as fast as you can
like a powerful
untamed horse
galloping away from pain.

Fly away from hate
on the wings of a dove
as the tips brush against the stars
leaving a trail of silver feathers.

Howl like a wolf on a lonely hill
as you cry at the moon about
your pain
shivering the cold air away.

Learn to be free.

MESSAGE TO MIKA

When you jolted our little worlds with your departure
you joined the wide universe
leaving us in various stages of shock therapy.

You made us look within and all around at one another
searching the "what ifs" and "if onlys."
But for the rest of the living world
it was like an electrical/elemental charge:

seeds newly planted sprouted on that day -
verbena, dahlias, asters, daisies, old geraniums
burst into an outrageous intensity of color
blazing in silent voices.

Now there are countless shards of your bright spirit
vibrating in the summer air
enough for all who knew you
or should have known you better.

You are a constant splinter in my heart
a bittersweet reminder of what love requires
carried like a talisman in wisps of song
exerting a gentle insistent force
to wake us from complacency.

6/26/04

ONCE

I have only met you once
But the connection was sure
A previous existence may be the tie
Your soul speaks to clarify your life
Through your eyes.

THE FLAME

She has turned off her reading light many years ago
Her eyes are straining to interpret the dialog
But there is no light to see
A candle flickers nearby, but there is no attempt to
Enhance her vision by the young glow
Instead she gets annoyed and tries to blow the flame out
The flame dances from side to side, pushed by the breath
Then grows from the strong air.

I LOVE THEM

I love them
I love them
Even if I am the only one who knows
I still will love them.

PRAYING FOR SANITY

Lord help me
I feel it caving in
My joys were polluted by the unwilling wind
He destroyed my word
He stroked my blind eye
He wore my love and never had it cleaned
Please help me regain my unfavorable spirit
The one that cannot be bared in this chaotic
And hypocritical age
I see him wanting me here
I see him thinking he is clean
But is he really
Are my eyes wrong to see the dirt flying with him
Do I really hear the deception of this twister
Or is it the jealous whisper of a deprived wave
Is the Earth sucking me down
While the wind is twisting me up
I don't know which it is
Or is it just me not looking up
Please don't get me wrong
Sometimes my spark is too hot
And I feel the heat rising to the gusts of insanity
And the flames being blown from bridge to bridge
But we all know that the only way for a fire
To get out of control is if there wind that is
Out of control.

The Sparrow -

A tiny bird whose sweet innocence
And life and death do not go unnoticed.

To Little Brother Jack, 4, from Kayla, 5

I love you Jack
I like to play with you
And I always like to sit by you
And I like to go see pictures of camels with you
And I like to do all things with you
And I like to play Santa Claus with you
And I like to play tent with you and motorcycles with you
And I like to play in the bath with you with all kinds of different toys
And I like to eat by you because I don't like to get scared by Michael Myers
And I like to take pictures of you
And I like to pretend we're doing magic
And I like to pretend magic eyeball
And I like to play Goldilocks
You're the guy that eats the porridge
And I like to eat candy and gum
And I like to eat pizza with M&M's on top
And I like to play video games at the pizza
And I like you to sleep with me
Because I'm afraid of Michael Myers
And I like to goof around because of Michael Myers
I like to play dolls with you
And I like to squeeze them.

Narrated by Kayla to Great Grandmother, Viv

ANGEL OF MINE

My love and I rise over a summit's glen
Where I make my vows known to her again.
To speak the language of hearts within,
Soaring as eagles, resurrecting in the wind.

I take these moments to etch the stars
With the promise of a future that is ours.
There will always be you "Angel of Mine"
None other ever could be as divine.

When I am close to you, I feel the smile of the light,
Of a million suns dancing, in all their might.
Time and space slip away into a lesser domain,
As infinitely the angelic chorus flow thru in sweet refrain.

HEAVENLY BIRDS

Two red birds winging it together
  In a forest of crystal snow.
Not feeling the chill or cold
  Because of their warm inner glow.
They haven't a worry or a care
  For theirs is an inner peace they share.
Never fearing if tomorrow will bring
  Storms from skies of grey.
For they live life to the fullest every day.

Some birds, like Jonathan Seagull,
  Venture as far as they can.
Then give their rewards to others,
  as a master plan

Heaven opens doors to those who fly high.
As "Birds of a Feather" we can too, if we try.

"Roughing it" at Christmas: The winter of 1981-1982

by

Marsha Fronefield

Donner Lake gets a lot of harsh weather. The area was named for a group of pioneers who were stranded in a September snowstorm and suddenly had to seek shelter from an unexpected early winter in the 1840's. They resorted to cannibalism in order to survive.

The winter of 1981-1982 also claimed lives. The day lodge at Alpine Meadows Ski Resort was destroyed in an avalanche. Five people died.

My work as the County health nurse tested my ability to deal with winter's challenges on the job, and at home.

We humans, however, are resilient. As time passes, memories fade and life goes on. T-shirts and bumper stickers sometimes result. Humor gets us through the bad times. "I survived the winter of 1981-1982" appeared predictably.

Another T-shirt of that era showed the aftermath of a long winter. It was created to supplement a meager student's income by "Michael Nahser-beam" and his friend Rick McGreevey, and was hawked in the streets of Berkeley, California.

The shirt depicted a drawing of "the day after the night before", with hungover partiers sprawled every which way. It's theme? "I survived the Donner Party".

A blizzard howled down out of the north in December 1981. Drifting snow piled so high, removing it was a creative process. Cars were stuck, plows were bogged down, and we literally threw shovelsful over our heads to get outside.

Truckee, Ca 1981-82

VR

"Cabin fever" set in with a vengeance. Tempers were short and about to become shorter.

We were watching "Close Encounters of the Third Kind", a story about humans meeting space aliens, with a young Richard Dreyfuss, when the power went out.

This was a common occurrence in these parts, and every mountain-savvy household kept candles, flashlights, lanterns, and lamp oil handy, as they still do, for such emergencies.

Books, board games, and playing cards were standard items for whiling away evenings when the lights went.

Couples frequently found other ways to pass the time. (a bumper crop of babies was born the following September.)

The next morning, the power was still out. I turned on the shower, and the <u>water</u> was gone, too. Not a drop! Not even what remained in the hot water tank.

After shoveling, and sweeping the snow off my Subaru, I headed into town for work.

As the "County Nurse", I had inside information: A transformer on Donner Summit was down, an ice storm had broken power lines, and with no electricity, the water pumps were gone as well. "The Summit" had even more snow, and it would probably take at least two weeks to restore utilities. Though the town of Truckee was not affected, outlying areas such as Donner Lake and subdivisions along the Truckee River were.

Workers would need skis and snow-cats (tractors) to reach the damage and make repairs, if the weather held.

To further complicate matters, Christmas was just three days away, and <u>we</u> were having the party at our house!

I asked Parky May, our local Red Cross representative, to open the middle school, which had heat, water, and power for showers and drinking water.

The Sheriff and Fire Department visited seniors, and needy families.

We filled every water container we could find at home.

Snow was melted on the wood burning stove, and (wonder of wonders!) we had propane to cook the Christmas ham and turkey.

There was no refrigerator, and no flush toilet. Innovation was on the short list of household priorities.

Time was running out, and we were convinced we'd have a large turnout for our Christmas bash. (a curious phenomenon occurs in small mountain towns: the worse the weather, the bigger the party. House-bound residents go to great lengths to attend festivities of all kinds, and flock to the restaurants.)

The ice chest on the back porch became our refrigerator. It had a lock to keep out "critters", and there was no need to visit the market for ice.

Attending to bathroom facilities was next. No flush toilet? No shower? No problem. We jury-rigged a shower from a camping device called a "Sun Shower". A five gallon bag with hose attached. The propane stove gave us our hot water.

A saucepan filled from a canning vat supplied water for a gravity flush. Water is simply dumped in the "bathroom bowl" to push contents through the sewer.

A flick of the wrist was the "secret technique" for the optimum flush.

We provided "Handi Wipes" for handwashing.

The storm had moved off, and Christmas Day dawned bright and sunny. No water, and no power, however. No music, and no drinks. Gin fizzes had been the plan, with Mimosas as backup, and soft drinks for children, and non-drinkers.

Kevin Shea, a DJ, brought a large battery operated "boom-box", and plenty of music.

Guests started arriving early and kept coming.

The problem with the gin fizzes was solved early on. We searched the cupboards for our largest mixing bowl. We used an eggbeater for a makeshift blender.

The water came back after ten days, the power in 14 days. The babies started coming the following September.

My friend, Norm, a psychologist, told me later, their son was born in September 1982. "You know, after the cable went out."

It took me a minute. "Oh."

                                                        ###

The Wild Horse

by

Vivian Hammond

When I picture the wild mustang I see them running in the Nevada desert high up in the hills, the powerful beautiful stallion chasing them from behind, their manes and tails flying and their voices singing in the wind. The lovely kiss of freedom written on their long history.

In the early 1800's it is said that there were about two million wild free mustangs in the United States. Other estimates are much higher. At one time they kept company alongside the buffalo grazing together on the Great Plains and other parts of the west. One by one most either died or were killed for food or slaughtered for dog food. Their numbers, although uncertain, are now only in the thousands.

At the dawn of their history a tiny, four toed creature (three on the back feet) about the size of a cat opened its large eyes and beheld the earth around it. Its scientific name was *Eohippus (a Greek word meaning "dawn horse")* and the earth upon which it stepped was the western United States. About fifty five million years ago. It is said that its evolution brought forth the modern horse, *Equus caballus*, that vanished from north America for eight thousand years before the new modern horse arrived, that had evolved elsewhere, and became the ancestors of today's horse. The mysterious disappearance of the horse during that period has been attributed to the arrival of early man who used it and the camel for food. Because of the complete extinction of the horse for those eight thousand years it also is speculated that a disease may have contributed to their demise. It seems logical, given this background, that the horse is actually a native of North America.

However, the mustang, is still classified as a *feral* animal, meaning a domestic stray, without the benefits of those animals classified as native. A benefit, for example, that would allow them to inhabit federal and state parks.

Some say the horse came to America by way of the Spanish conquistadores who, when retreating, left horses behind that became wild and multiplied. Others say the wild horse came from ranches near the Mexico border that were sometimes raided by Indians and the horses were left to scatter and become wild. Both may be true. And other explanations as well. The mustang's ancestry goes back to Arabian, Barb, Andalusia, the Spanish horse, Jenets and others. J. Frank Dobie, in his book, "The Mustang", gives an excellent account of the arrival and ancestry of the horse coming to America.

The mustang is usually a small horse, from 13 to 15 hands, from 700 to 1000 pounds. Many are pony size. Some anthropologists think that their stature is nature's way of preserving them by having a small body that requires less food to survive. Mustangs, taken out of the wild and cared for with a rich steady diet, have produced larger offspring than themselves.

The color of the mustang varies. It's long history has a mixed bloodline going back centuries from the Spanish horse to domestic horses that were tempted to follow wild herds. The predominant color appears to be dun or a "lively light brown". The Appalosoa was patiently developed by the Nez Perce Indians and has the unique spotted rump.

Nature gave the mustang the instinct not to inbreed. When an offspring turns about two years old they are driven off from the herd of their parents by the stallion and have to go their own way sometimes forming little adolescent bands of their own that may trail behind the main herd.

A mustang stallion will many times fight to the death to keep another younger stallion from stealing his mares. It doesn't matter that some of his mares may not be attractive, being old, decrepid or injured. And, should his mares wander off, the stallion will find them and harass them until they return. If they protest he "bites" them and herds them back. He mostly follows his band from behind and herds them, circling to keep them all together. A lead mare usually points the way ahead and the others follow.

It is a peculiar thing that a stallion may be inclined to choose his mares by color and sometimes a whole band will be the same color. He may be black but all of his mares may be a cream color.

It is without question that the horse changed the lives and culture of early native Americans. At first they were terrified of the man and horse together that could separate from each other without pain. Eventually, the "big dog" became an integral part of their societies. The horse changed their lives forever. It was held in such awe that it was, for years, used only for hunting, warring and in ceremonies. The squaws, children and dogs still walked, carrying or dragging their belongings behind them. The horse allowed the Indians to plunge into herds of buffalo for the kill. Food was now easier to come by. Their enemies feared the Indians with horses for they could now strike far and wide.

Without the horse the West could not have been explored or settled as it was. The new Americans owe the horse a debt that can never be repaid.

The cowboy often took more than one horse from the wild to train as his own knowing the little horse's ability to maneuver in the cattle herds and their stamina on the long cattle drives.

The slaughter of the wild horse, although continuous, was the probably the worst in a four year period after World War II when a 100,000 horses were taken from Nevada alone by the use of airborne vehicles.

It was a fateful day in 1950 when Velma Johnston, the famed Wild Horse Annie, followed a truck down Highway 395 to Reno that appeared to have live animals inside. She realized a stream of blood was coming from the bed of the truck leaving a trail on the highway. Curiously, she followed it. When it stopped she could see the truck was packed full of horses, many wounded and bleeding, a colt lie on the floor crushed to a pulp, the stallion was blind. His eyes had been shot out. The fate of these horses was in a slaughterhouse somewhere, to be made into dog food. This experience so impacted her that she spent years of her life pushing for legislation on a state and federal level to protect the mustang.

In 1959 Congress passed the "Wild Horse Annie" bill protecting feral horses from being hunted by aircraft or motorized vehicles on the

From "Sweet Promised Land" by Robert Laxalt

"And what an outfit it was," he said, with still a little amazement in his voice. "We ran nearly twenty thousand head of sheep and a few thousand cattle, and we owned wonderful grazing land for fifty miles. We had dozens of herders and buckaroos and so many saddle horses that we never used them all. We brought in our supplies by the truckloads and we even had a store on the ranch where the workingmen could check out anything they wanted against their wages, things like levis and work shirts and jumpers and gloves and tobacco.

We owned Cadillacs and when we went to Reno we rented rooms and apartments, and we ate with bankers, and in the saloons we treated the house every time we had a drink." He shook his head. "Sometimes, thinking back, I can't hardly believe it. It was a time like I'd never seen in America before, and never saw again."

"And then," he said, nodding heavily, "the market began to go. At first, everyone said it was just a little slump, and that it would be over with in a hurry. But it wasn't just a slump. It was the end. Before you could even turn around, sheep and cattle weren't worth anything, and you couldn't have sold if you wanted to, because nobody would buy any."

He put his hands to his eyes. "It was the saddest thing to see," he said. "We couldn't even make the interest payments on the mortgages, much less the principal. And then, the bankers started coming out to the camps and the ranches again, but this time they didn't smile very much. First, they began to take the grazing land and the stock, and then they took the ranch itself. They wouldn't even let me keep my beautiful black stallion horse that I had broken and raised myself and that nobody else had ever ridden, and it did my heart good afterward when I found out that the first time they tried to ride him he threw the rider and the saddle and everything and ran away wild to the hills he came from."

Dominique Laxalt

public domain. This cruel method of rounding up wild horses forced the running horses to fall down from exhaustion, their unshod hooves worn off and bleeding and often blinded from shotgun blasts from the planes as well as foals left motherless and unprotected from predators. Some horses, blinded from the shotguns, were left to wander helplessly and starve. Velma Johnston's untiring efforts raised the consciousness of legislators and the common people alike. This law was later amended to allow the BLM to round up mustangs by aircraft to establish their control.

On December 15, 1971 President Nixon signed PL 92-195 designating the wild horse "a national heritage species and an esthetic resource" into law.

The first paragraph reads:

Be it enacted by the Senate and House of Representatives of the United States of America in Congress assembled, That Congress finds and declares that wild free-roaming horses and burros are living symbols of the historic and pioneer spirit of the West; that they contribute to the diversity of live forms within the Nation and enrich the lives of the American people; and that these horses and burros are fast disappearing from the American scene. It is the policy of Congress that wild free-roaming horses and burros shall be protected from capture, branding, harassment, or death; and to accomplish this they are to be considered in the area where presently found, as an integral part of the natural system of the public lands.

Other legislation is being introduced in 2005 but, at this writing, has not been signed into law.

A documentary on the Discovery Channel in March of 2004 describes the journey taken by wild horses that exceed those numbers that can exist on the land.

A (BLM) Bureau of Land Management contractor rounds up the mustangs by helicopter and funnels them into pens. The stallions are kept separate. In Palamino Valley, Nevada, there are facilities to hold 2,000 horses. They are brought there, given physicals, a freeze mark is put on them (not a brand) and they are monitored for a month. Some stallions are too old to be tamed and are let back into the wild.

In Wheatland, Wyoming there is a "horse whisperer" and horse trainer for the BLM. He apparently tames and trains part of the herd.

In Riverton, Wyoming there is an honor camp for prison inmates. About one hundred fifty are involved in the "taming" not "training" of the mustangs. Many times a bond forms between horse and man and it is a hard thing for both of them when they must separate.

The last phase of this documentary spoke of Phoenix, Arizona where the adoption process takes place. Owners are carefully screened. If a horse is adopted and evidence shows that they are being neglected, they are taken back.

Untamed horses go for about $125.00. If it is obvious that a horse has a high percentage of Spanish blood they go for much higher. The highest amount, they recalled, went for $19,000.00.

Older horses not adopted are sent to sanctuaries in Oklahoma and Kansas.

Controversy has surrounded the very existence of the mustang. Many ranchers and cattlemen believe that the food on the rangelands belong to their cattle and the mustang threaten that food supply. Some of them believe that the slaughter of the mustang is a good thing. Other ranchers allow the mustangs on their own land and hide their knowledge that horses are even there to protect them.

In the 1961 film "The Misfits", written by Arthur Miller, with Clark Gable, Marilyn Monroe, Montgomery Clift, Eli Wallach and Thelma Ritter, gives a very thoughtful account of the plight of the mustang during that period.

At one point Gable explains to Marilyn that the mustangs are 'misfits', small but with enormous stamina. When Marilyn realizes what was about to take place with the rounding up of six mustangs that will be slaughtered for dog food, she erupts, running into desert, "Murderers," she cries.

The three men, Gable, Clift and Wallach who all of their adult lives seemed to have avoided "working for wages" in ordinary jobs, have survived from rodeos, mustanging and who knows what else. This gentle, caring woman who has just entered their lives, who is also beautiful, has wiggled her way into their hearts and minds. They each think they have a chance with her. "You have the gift of life," Gable says to her.

Monroe says, "I can't stand for anything to get killed …you know what you are doing isn't right."

In a very remarkable, violent, one on one scene, between Gable and the stallion, the strength and determination between animal and man becomes a bloody fight for their freedom, in which man prevails. In the end all of the animals are let go mostly because of the tears and empathy Monroe shows for these beautiful animals. Gable and Clift are moved to change their lives. Wallach, who remains steeped in his own demons, goes on as always.

In 2005, in Nevada, there is an estimate of 19,000 mustangs. The estimate in ten western United States is 35,000.

In early August, 2004, this author decided to go where I was told there were some mustangs and see them for myself. I was told that there were mustangs in the Virginia Highlands, a mountainous region near Virginia City, Nevada. I remembered on my infrequent sojourns to Virginia City seeing a sign to my left saying "Virginia City Highlands". Sojourns mostly to entertain company from the Bay Area.

I was, in fact, reluctant to even buy film for the small trip knowing that, if my luck ran true, I would probably not see anything much less take pictures.

I put extra gas in my white 1995 Jeep Grand Cherokee, with 3 small dents and a hole in its black plastic bumper. I did buy a roll of film with 24 prints at 7-11 a few minutes from my house in Washoe Valley.

And so I went where I had never gone before.

After first entering the paved road after the "Virginia City Highlands" sign, I noticed a dirt road to my right after only driving about a half mile. I took it and drove into the wild, sort of, until it ended in a dead end. A few barnlike houses were here and there along with steep ravines and woods. But no mustangs.

Onward. Virginia City Highlands is a Nevada style Oakland Hills with many, many barnlike houses that cost "God knows how much", with Hummers, convertibles and other similar vehicles in their driveways. Some had small corrals with one or two horses. Miles and

miles went by and still more expensive barnlike houses.

I saw a few signs that said something like "Don't feed or harass the wild horses". I made note that if I were to see some, I wouldn't do that.

At last I came upon a Fire Station. I drove in to inquire about my mission. A young thin man was outside. I told him I was interested in taking pictures of mustangs and did he know where I might find them. "Well, they are kind of everywhere," he said. "We see them all the time. There is a couple over there." He pointed across from me at a large house and I realized that, sure enough, two horses, beautiful chestnuts, were meandering up the tree strewn hillside towards the house.

I immediately jumped in my jeep and scooted over there. They seemed to not pay any attention to me and I got a couple of photos even though only part of their bodies were visible through the bushes and trees. I'm sure the young fireman that I had met thought I was very weird.

I intended to go forward on this same road but I was met with a sign saying, "Private Road, No Trespassing" or something of that nature. I then drove over to the road by the Fire House to go down that road and was met with a similar sign. The very rich can own everything, I decided.

The only road left to access was a right turn on the road I had originally come in from. And, left with no options, I struck out again. More barnlike, rich houses on both sides. Where could these mustangs be I had heard about?

I drove slowly observing any vacant land I could see and occasionally a car or jeep would barrel past me impatiently. Some with teens just old enough to drive, a scent of cigarette smoke from their open windows along with music and loud talking.

At last the rich barnlike houses became fewer and fewer. And then there were none. I emerged into a large valley with an occasional tree and lots of sagebrush and other low plant life. It appeared to be somewhat flat but I was to later learn that it, in fact, had a rolling sort of aspect, with many long depressions in it. As I rode along the main road I suddenly encountered, to my left, a long seemingly endless dirt road that led across the valley and up to the top of the mountain. I stopped dead in my tracks. Then I turned into it looking for the sign telling me I couldn't.

No such sign existed.

About a half mile in from the main road there was a rather large house, only slightly barnlike, with a modern windmill turning lazily in the wind and half of a large rack of solar panels in front of the house. I also noticed in the back there was a volleyball net set up which sort of took me aback. I wondered who on earth could live there.

I slowed to a stop when I noticed a dark horse grazing near the house. There were no fences anywhere that I could see and the horse seemed unconcerned that I was there although I was being very unobtrusive by driving very slowly and quietly. I stopped and decided that this had to be a mustang. I got out of the car and took pictures of him. I noticed several long scars on his back. He glanced up at me now and then and continued to graze. I spent so much time in his presence that I began to enjoy his quiet company.

After awhile I decided to follow the dirt road all the way to the top because I thought maybe I was hot on the trail of a herd of mustangs and that the stallion I had just taken pictures of was their leader. It never occurred to me in reality that I was right.

The road was terrible. Narrow, rutted, strewn with rocks and steeper and steeper. I put my jeep in first gear which I don't ever remember doing before. I talked to myself, encouraging myself to go on, so that maybe my dream of seeing a herd of mustangs would actually come true.

And then came the crest of the hill. I could not believe what I was looking at. Another expensive barnlike house!!! I have to admit I said a few bad words. Nobody, thank goodness, was home.

I looked out over the other side of the small mountain and far below I saw a settlement that I was not able to identify. Just a large pattern of roads and houses like a big orderly jigsaw puzzle.

I walked over by my car and looked out toward the valley from which I had just come and raised my new binoculars to my eyes. What I saw was so overwhelming I was afraid my urinary tract would refrain from doing what it was supposed to be doing. There, just beyond the house, was a whole band of mustangs, multi-colored, dark, white and tan. Eight, maybe ten. Gently walking and grazing not far from the stallion going in the direction away from the road. I could hardly contain myself.

I, of course, got in my jeep and proceeded down the terrible, narrow road as best I could. By the time I got there and got out of my car and stood up on the space by the door, they were far away. With my binoculars I counted eight. They seemed healthy and beautiful. Even though I was sad not to get a good picture, I felt lucky to see them.

I wanted a picture of them so badly that I struck out into the desert to look for them, leaving the sanctuary of my car. A couple of football fields away seeing nothing with my binoculars, I saw a movement out of the corner of my eye. I froze as I saw what it was. A wolf. For some weird reason I turned and took a picture of it. Before I die, I thought. I talked softly to it and as it got closer I realized that it had on a collar and a dog license. But that didn't seem to matter at the moment because it would not stop coming towards me. I moved slowly away talking to it and it moved with me. In fact, it accompanied me all the way back to my car, parallel to me about 20 feet away to my right. When I got back to my car I was so grateful at not being attacked I left him a little pile of potato chips near my car, which he ignored, and continued to escort me as I drove past the house towards the main road.

A small truck was coming up the road and I stopped as it approached and it stopped, too. It was a young handsome Indian man with a beautiful smile. I told him what I was up to and he said, "Oh yeah, they were just here and now their gone. I don't know where."

So he, evidently, was the owner of the house. How appropriate, I thought.

For some hours after that I climbed back up the mountain searching more and more for the small band but they had eluded me, maybe in a depression of earth or under one of the few trees or up into the wooded hills. I don't know.

Broomtail, Cayuse, Mestenos, Mustang - each name may hold slightly different connotations but they are still the same wild horse that mysteriously took their freedom and have held it for centuries in spite of settlers, fences, cattlemen, mustangers, little food, freezing winters and blazing hot summers. They are both loved and hated but still belong to a part of this earth's landscape just as man does.

                                                                    ###

Lucy, I'm Home

by

Rick Hammond

My name is Rickey Lynn Hammond, but I go by Rick Hammond, or just Rick. Researching a paper for English 101, I decided to ask my mother how I got my name. She regretfully responded, "Well, I named you after Ricky Ricardo from the "I Love Lucy" television show." My response was "Oh". Then, as I was putting myself back together, it hit me all at once. All my life, people have been calling me "Ricky Ricardo" or just "Ricardo". I should have guessed I was named after a fictional T.V. character. I love my mother very much, so I have forgiven her. She was only eighteen years of age when I was born.

Now, having learned all this, every time someone calls my name, I will very likely hear the song "Babaloo" (a song made popular by Ricky Ricardo in the 1950's) shoot through my head like a silver bullet. Of course, the character of Ricky was played by a Cuban immigrant who shortened his name from Desiderio Alberto Arnazy de Archa III to Desi Arnaz. I wonder if I would be answering to the name "Desi", if he had used his real first name on the T.V. show.

I recall seeing a very drunk Desi Arnaz on the Steve Allen television show several years ago. I laughed hysterically watching him make a fool of himself, being rude to the other guests, and playing a conga drum with Mr. Allen's band. I'm not so sure I would laugh so hard now.

I didn't know where my name came from until now, and I'm forty-four years old. I never liked my name enough to ask about it. To me, Rickey Lynn sounded like a girl name, and boys with girl names didn't do well where I grew up. When I was about ten years old, I began telling people my name was Rick, leaving out the "ey", it sounded so girlish. I would allow only my grandmother to call me Rickey, and she does to this day.

Some people wrongly assume my name is Richard, which is sometimes shortened to Rick. Some Richards are referred to as Dick. When asked if my name (Rick) was short for Richard, I would sometimes say "yes" but I was much younger then. I've been asked, "So, your name is Richard. Mind if I call you Dick?" My immediate response would be "Yes, I do mind, my name is Rick."

I was occasionally teased, because of my name rhyming with a word some people use referring to a male body part, and my feelings would be hurt. I've been referred to as "Slick' and it always felt like a warm pat on the back. When people want to give me a hard time, they come up with all kinds of rhymes for my name (ick, lick, pick, chick, etc.).

I can't recall anyone addressing me as Rickey Lynn, to my face. I might have responded well in my early years. Nowadays, I don't think it's so bad. I am a guitar player and a name like Rickey Lynn Hammond sounds like a pretty good stage name. But there's already a Stevie Ray Vaughn and a Kenny Wayne Shepherd (famous guitar players) and I would like to be an original. I'll bet neither of them were named after a fictional T.V. character, and Ricky Ricardo was a bandleader long before they were.

RICKEY LYNN

RICKEY

I asked my mother about my middle name (Lynn). Her response was, "I took it from a guy at my high school, he was very popular, his name was Lynn Wheeler." I asked my mom if he was her boyfriend. She said, "No, actually, I never talked to him." She had a secret crush on him. She said to never tell my dad. They've been divorced thirty-eight years.

What's in a name? Sometimes too much.

###

Rick

Give Unto Others

by

Julia Dodd

Mattie Oberholtzer was a recluse. It happened gradually after Henry, her husband of forty years, died. At first she stopped going to church, although she still prayed every night on her knees before going to bed. She also sometimes talked to Henry telling him the events of the day which were not much usually. Of course, Henry never talked back. In life or in death. Then she didn't go out at night. She bought all the groceries her little cart could carry holding off going to the grocery store. Then she began not answering the door and the phone. Unless it rang and rang, which drove her crazy. Five years ago she stopped her annual visits to her children's in California. She stopped inviting them to her place. The only mail she opened were bills. At eighty-one she had lived far longer than she had planned. Both spiritually and financially.

Her old wrinkled face couldn't compare to the beauty she saw on TV every day. She began to think of herself as very ugly. With the quiet erosion of her confidence came a deep, hurting loneliness. In her private world she never talked, except to Henry, and was never touched.

Then one blustery September day the phone rang and rang. Finally, she picked it up.

"Mrs. Oberholtzer?"

"Yes."

"This is Mrs. Briggs with the Cancer Society. We need your help this year."

Mattie blinked behind her horn rims. "Well, I usually give a dollar to Mrs. Stover." Mrs. Stover always stayed on the porch until Mattie answered the door, stubbornly.

"I'm so sorry to tell you this but Mrs. Stover caught the flu last March and died."

"Oh," Mattie hadn't heard. "Poor old soul."

"I was hoping you could take over for her. There's only five houses on your street besides Mr. Bickett's. You wouldn't have to go there. It wouldn't take you twenty minutes and it would be such a relief to me. I just got out of the hospital ...."

Mattie tried to say no. Every time she tried, Mrs. Briggs had some reason why she couldn't do it herself. A much more important reason than Mattie could think up. At the end of the phone call, it was suddenly all arranged. Mattie was going to do it.

In three weeks she had not been out of the house. With a weeks worth of food left she had no intention of going out. Yet she had been out-talked by Mrs. Briggs. Committing herself.

Well, maybe she would just pretend to do it. If she could spare five dollars she would just put in a dollar for each house. She found her purse hanging in the closet. It was the last of the month. Eight days before her Social Security check would be put into her checking account at the bank. Her small pension check from Henry had long ago gone for the rent. She had eight dollars and twenty cents.

Mrs. Briggs came the next day with the paraphernalia with which Mattie was to do her collecting. Something unexpected. A little bookkeeping card with a place for names, addresses and amounts given by each family.

"Just forget about collecting from Mr. Bickett. He hasn't ever given and never will. Now it could be some people might not be home." Mrs. Briggs had a very musical, loud voice. "If that happens just leave this envelope with this little paper in it and hopefully they will send it in."

Mattie was relieved to hear this.

"Of course, that's not likely for more than one or two houses."

Mattie nodded wearily. Mrs. Briggs was a foot taller than Mattie. Hardly forty, she had wild red hair and chestnut eyes that could probably see a mile. Mattie had trouble seeing the children on the sidewalk going back and forth to school. She remembered how it was to be a child. Her senses sharp. Everything brand new. Even she was new. Shyly stepping into the world. Still shy.

"Let's see, it's Tuesday." Mrs. Briggs was looking about Mattie's small living room as if in search of a calendar. Mattie self-consciously remembered that she hadn't dusted the piano or the children's and grand-children's pictures in two weeks. "I'll come by Saturday afternoon. That should be plenty of time. Too bad about Mrs. Stover. She usually collected at least ten dollars. I'm sure you'll do just fine."

Mattie choked. Ten dollars.

When Mrs. Briggs left Mattie started walking the floor. How did she get herself into this puzzle?

By Friday morning she was in a state. Not one penny had she collected. She had, by now, eaten her chicken pot pies, her cereal, milk and hamburger. The last of the toilet paper had unrolled this morning. As she watched the children go by, walking in the rain, she tried to calculate what to do.

Two things were for sure. She needed names and addresses for the five houses and she needed to go to the store.

After her bath, she put her collecting paraphernalia in her purse, donned her coat and umbrella and reluctantly set out for the store pulling her little shopping cart behind her.

In the store she got mixed up on her spending. To her horror the few things she bought came to five dollars and seven cents. Too embarrassed to take anything back, she paid it. On the way home she studied the register receipt and the contents of the bag inside the wire shopping cart. For one thing she had meant to only buy one roll of toilet paper. Instead, without thinking, she had gotten a four-pack. Her other little mistakes made up the rest. Now she had three dollars and thirteen cents left.

The first house that she would need the address from was only three down from her own. It had a chain link fence around it about four feet high with rosebushes intertwined in it. The mailbox was by the front gate. Fumbling nervously, she got out her little bookkeeping card and started writing.

To reassure herself she glanced up at the window. A woman was looking right back at her. She almost fainted when she saw her.

Young and sassy looking. Mattie was about to take off when the door opened.

"You want something?" She talked sassy, too.

Mattie was sure that if her old blood could have rushed to her cheeks that it probably did.

"I -- have to collect for Cancer this year." She was stumbling. "Mrs. Stover died."

Sassy smiled. A remarkably beautiful smile. "Oh, I thought you were a bill collector or something. Hang on a minute." She soon came out in the rain with two dollar bills in her hand. "Sorry to hear about that old lady. I never knew her name. She was nice. You take care, now. Don't walk out in this rain too much. You might get a cold."

"Oh, no I won't. Thank you." Self consciously, Mattie took the two dollars, smiled and walked on.

Sassy hurried back inside.

My Lord, Mattie thought, only eight dollars to go. When she got to the next house it seemed like a million. As fast as she could, she managed to write down the name and address from the mailbox. Being mistaken for a bill collector was something she didn't want to repeat. An old car was parked in the driveway. For a long moment she hesitated. If only Henry were still alive. She could have followed him in. Let him do the asking. But Henry was gone.

No Salesmen or Solicitors, a tin sign read on one of the porch posts. It was a little sign. Until she was already on the porch, she hadn't seen it. When she did, she turned on her heels. In her haste one foot got hooked around the other. Hovering for a moment, she fell off the porch and landed in a heap. Her heavy coat had acted like a cushion.

The door of the house came open. An old man, as tall as the door itself, stood there glaring down at her.

"You trying to kill yourself?"

Mattie was trying to get herself together enough to get up. Her ankle felt funny. "I didn't see your sign right off."

When she tried to get all the way up she had to grab for the porch post to keep from falling again. As best she could, she lowered herself down to sit on the step. All the while the old man watched.

"Did you go and break something?"

Mattie was on the verge of blubbering. "I think my ankle."

He walked down the steps and looked down at her swelling ankle. "Now, I suppose you're going to sue me."

That was it. She did blubber. The gates burst wide open.

"Now, now. Don't be crying, woman. I know you wouldn't do it on purpose. You're just old and clumsy, that's all. Now quit your crying."

She felt worse. Old, yes. Clumsy, never. When she finally managed to squelch the last sob, she got mad. "You're as old as I am." She snapped off the words. "Probably older."

His old face crinkled into a smile. "Maybe. Not as clumsy, though. Not by a long shot."

Mattie blinked up at him trying to conquer a new flood coming up in her throat. He leveled a pair of blue eyes on her from an old weather-beaten face.

"Well, do you have a doctor?"

"Dr. Marcus."

"Stay here. I'll be right back."

So she sat there in the rain. Swelling and crying, swearing she would never leave her home again.

She could hear him growling inside the house.

When he came back out he took her under the arms and lifted her up. All hundred pounds of her. "Let's go."

"Where?"

"Doctor's office."

Awkwardly, he helped her into his old car. He had strong hands, she thought, warm.

Two hours went by before the old car puttered back into Radby Circle. Mattie's ankle was wrapped. Crutches lay in the back seat all adjusted to her size. She was exhausted.

"I'll get you into your house." The old man was saying. He did and left.

A few minutes later she heard a knock. Her front door opened. It was him.

"Just me. I brought over your groceries. You left them out on the sidewalk."

"Oh, thank you."

He walked by her sitting on the couch into the kitchen. She could hear him putting things away.

When he came into the living room he was carrying her collecting stuff. "This was all over my porch."

Wearily she took it from him. "Too bad Mrs. Stover died," she said sadly. "She always collected at least ten dollars."

"Do-good women." He was writing on the back of one of the envelopes. "Here's my number in case you fall down and break the other one."

Mrs. Briggs came the next afternoon. Mattie was sitting on the couch with her leg up, depressed.

"You poor thing." Her chestnut eyes got really big when she came in. "What happened?"

Mattie told her. "I'm sorry, Mrs. Briggs. I didn't do all my collecting." Mattie thought she might cry but she held on. She couldn't tell Mrs. Briggs that it had taken her until Friday to screw up the courage.

"Well, let me see here." She took Mattie's collecting stuff. "Well, uh-huh. Uh. Well, for goodness sake."

Mattie tried to see what warranted a "goodness sake" but couldn't.

"I don't know how you did it. Mr. Bickett must me softening up a little. Actually gave this year."

Mattie blinked. "Mr. Bickett?"

"Well, while I'm here I'll go to the other houses. You get well now. We'll need your help next year. Mrs. Oberholtzer, thank you for caring. We need your kind of people."

"Thank you." Mattie felt a little breeze of pride pass over her. Mr. Bickett? Now, she remembered the name on the mailbox. He had been so crotchety and insulting. No wonder Mrs. Stover never asked him more than once what with his sign and all. But he had taken her to the doctor. He had given her a donation. Out of pity, no doubt.

That afternoon, just as Mattie was thinking that her life had gotten back to normal, the phone rang and rang. It was him.

"Do you like fish?"

"Well, yes."

"Caught a couple of big ones this morning. I'll cook them up for supper for the two of us. I can't eat all of them anyway. No sense in your trying to cook on those crutches."

"Well, uh ..."

"See you this evening about five."

When he hung up she kept on thinking about him. Never giving to Mrs. Stover and all. He had seen Mattie's bare cupboards and refrigerator. Maybe, she thought, his sharing with her was really his kind of charity. Closer to home.

It was nice to know he would be coming over. Henry would have liked him. They would have talked about fishing.

Sitting near the phone she began to think about how the grand-children must have grown by now. She wondered about her children, Charlie and Pam. So busy they were. So important in their jobs. She felt warm when she thought of them. Being with people had been hard. Still it had gone all right. Maybe she would just call and say hello.

###

NOTES FROM OUR CONTRIBUTORS

Margaret Fago - Artist - Cover
Watercolorist Margaret W. Fago is making her mark as a marine artist. She has long had an interest in boats, boating and water subjects, both as an artist and as a sailor. She has paintings in a number of private collections both in the USA and Abroad.

Chris Hammond I - Artist - The Pony
I don't usually have much time to draw but when I do, I enjoy it. Besides, anything for my Mom.

Vivian Hammond - Writer, Editor, Publisher
I have been writing since I was nine. I used to write while sitting in a walnut tree in front of our house in Napa, California. I think I was considered a little weird but nobody seemed to mind. And although I no longer sit in a tree while writing, I look back fondly at the pure thoughts I had in those days. I now sit in front of a computer and gaze out the window at the sunrise. Nothing much has changed.

Special permission was given by Monique Laxalt, the daughter of Robert Laxalt, to quote from his book "Sweet Promised Land" in the essay "The Wild Horse". Thank you.

Kim Henrick - Writer
Kim Henrick has lived in western Nevada for nearly 50 years. She prefers dogs to people, quiet to crowds, dirt roads to blacktop, trailer towns to gated communities and laughter to therapy. The best advice she ever received on writing and life came from a bumper sticker: *Grin like a dog and wander aimlessly.*

Jay Reed - Poet and Poetry Editor
Jay Reed is a lifelong poet masquerading as an over-the-hill (and dale) process server and courier. Mother of five and grandmother of three, she lives among the redwoods in western Sonoma County (CA) and enjoys reading when not traveling around the country on essential errands.

Mika Drew - Poet
Granddaughter of Jay Reed. A young angel.

Kayla Hammond - Poet
At five years old, she is an aspiring poet and kindergartner.

April Jeanne Hammond - Poet
Since I can remember, I have always understood that my true home is with my creator. In that separation there has been a process taking place with elements of grief, anxiety, understanding, coping and throughout all, love. Having children at a young age exposed me more fiercely to the ways of the world and I would have it no other way. My boys helped me to have transcendental vision in which I try to apply to my life daily. They have helped me to recognize that all communication is a gesture or cry for love. My writing is always reflecting this. My journals or poetry is my way of coping with my separation or my possession of the source of love, God.

James Keith - Poet
Exploring ancient mythology since 8th grade, I learned how the law of today had roots steered in former traditions, leading back to folklore. Having an open mind, yet remaining skeptical, led me to write poetry, song lyrics, sing and play the guitar and invent electronics. Often there is a current of discontinuity pulling us away from harmony with each other. "Love" opens the door for wisdom, when we are then ready to handle true power, to attain freedom. We must find ways to connect with each other; like one song-bird singing to another. Love is universal and (often) expressed in music and poetry. Having insights about my "enchanting" wife, Carol, I wrote her many poems. I called her "Angel" and still do. An Ohio 'Red Bird', I now enjoy living in Reno, Nevada.

Carol Keith - Poet

Born in Ohio, I spent my early years as a vocalist in the Midwest and New York, performing in night clubs, and then the talk show host (I originated) for W.E.W.S. in Cleveland, Ohio. California bound, a few years later, I met Jim in Pasadena and then married in Kauai, HA. Then Broadcast Training in Hollywood. Then I formed a K.C.L.A. Radio Talk Show with Jim, as my Co-Host, airing for 3 1/2 years. Soon we discovered we both hailed from Ohio; symbol of the "Red Bird". Many cards to each other followed, displaying the "Red Birds". So I decided to write a Love Poem about us, thus the title: "Two Red Birds". These Red Birds, now living in Reno, are busy working on a *form of* (patent pending) lighting technology.

Marsha Fronefield - Writer

Marsha Sidwell-Fronefield has lived in the mountains most of her life. As a child, she lived in Big Bear and Crestline in Southern California. Truckee, California became her home in her adult years. She currently lives in Verdi, Nevada with her husband, Mike, and their dog and cat. She has been writing all her life, and is now working on a project - "How I Met The Love Of My Life".

Rick Hammond - Writer

Thinking about my life and looking back, there have been extreme changes. My lifestyle and my point of view, have been altered by the lessons I have learned. It doesn't necessarily mean that I have wavered. It's just an ongoing awareness. Memories of my childhood and the people who were my parents and are my parents, give my life some meaning. The year is 2006. I was born in 1955. Between that time and this, the world has changed more dramatically than ever before. Yet there are still things that give me comfort of familiarity; Motorcycles, Family, Guitars and Fishing. This is who I am.

Julia Dodd - Writer
Julia Dodd describes herself as an old coot who lives in the Nevada countryside with one dog, three chickens, and two little rambunctious kids, who, on occasion, sits down and precariously writes a story.

2006 - Our prayers are again with our sons and daughters who have bravely left our America to fight in Iraq and will come home. For those who lost their precious lives there, Godspeed.